My Veggetti
SPIRAL
Vegetable
Cookbook

My Veggetti
SPIRAL
Vegetable
Cookbook

Spiralizer cutter recipes to inspire your Low Carb, Paleo, Gluten-free and Healthy Eating Lifestyle

For All Vegetable Spaghetti Pasta Makers and Slicers

STACY HILL

DISCLAIMER

The publisher and author make no representations or warranties with respect to the accuracy or completeness of the contents of this work and specially disclaim all warranties, including warranties without limitation warranties of fitness for a particular purpose. No warranties may be created or extended by sales or promotions. The information and strategies herein may not be suitable for every situation. This material is sold with the understanding that the author or publisher is not engaged in rendering medical, legal, or other professional advice or services. If professional help is required, the services of a competent professional should be sought. Neither the publisher nor the author shall be liable for damages arising here from. The fact that an individual or organisation is referred to in this work as a citation and/or possible source of further information or resource does not mean the author or the publisher endorses the information of the individual or organisation that they/it may provide or recommend.

Many of the designations used by manufacturers and sellers to distinguish their products are claimed as trademarks. Any and all product names referenced within this book are the trademarks of their respective owners. None of these owners have sponsored, endorsed or approved this book. Always read all information provided by the manufacturer's product labels or manuals before using their products. The author and publisher are not responsible for product claims made by manufacturers.

MALIBU PRESS

ISBN-13: 978-1505440089
ISBN-10: 1505440084

TABLE OF CONTENTS

VEGGETTI HAS CHANGED MY LIFE!

For most of my life, I've spent a lot of time thinking about food and coming up with new recipe ideas. Therefore if someone had asked me about my hobby, honestly, I would have to say it's fooding. Yes, fooding is my hobby. Ouch! I know, "fooding" is not an official word in the English Language, but out of my passion for food, I've finally decided to invent my own word. Ahahah. Well, as a foodie, it was no wonder that I had overdone it a bit and gained some extra pounds. Fortunately, the pounds didn't stay after my discovery of an irresistibly handy kitchen gadget known as the Veggetti. Now I can say that the Veggetti has helped me to easily prepare healthier low carb meals. It has changed my life! Now, I can't imagine cooking without it.

Back when I first bought my Veggetti, I had no idea how much it would have helped to significantly improve my health. But it did! By turning my vegetables into spaghetti, I am eating healthier than before. Only then, did losing weight become easier and realistic. For this reason, I can concur that by ditching regular carb and fat laden pasta dishes for one that is totally low carb and nutritious, you'd be amazed at the results. It works and it's easy!

Remarkably, I've come to realize that preparing really healthy and delicious food doesn't have to be complicated and time-consuming. What's even more interesting is that creating vegetable spiral dishes using the Veggetti hasn't taken the fun out of my cooking. Even my kids have become interested in my Veggetti dishes.

In this cookbook, I am excited to share some of my personal "go-to" Veggetti inspired recipes. So, if you need to create some good-for-you recipes with your spiral shredder or cutter, this book is for you. You'll be able to create a variety of healthy and delicious recipes with your vegetable spaghetti.

Now I must admit that I don't want to be a skinny missy—it's just not me. But, I will never go back to being that heavy again, even though I still love fooding around.

WHY THIS COOKBOOK

This cookbook presents a variety of fresh and delicious recipes for your Veggetti spiralizer. The book is specially created with a new collection of good-for-you recipes which also includes recipes that are Paleo friendly, gluten-free and dairy-free. Moreover, these recipes are all low-carb, high fiber and low-fat and are geared towards supporting a healthy lifestyle. Consequently, you will find this book to be particularly helpful if you are looking for delicious Veggetti recipes for:

✓ Low Carb Diet
✓ Gluten-Free Diet
✓ Paleo Diet
✓ Dairy-Free Diet
✓ Overall Good Health

Considering all this, by using these low

carb recipes you would be enhancing your health with inspiring Veggetti spiralizer recipes. With the easy-to-get ingredients and simple directions in this book, you'll be able to easily create healthy and flavorful meals in a jiffy.

VEGGETTI SPIRALIZER 101

The Veggetti spiralizer is used in a similar way to how you would use a pencil sharpener. It's just that instead of sharpening a pencil, you would be sharpening your vegetable to create curly noodle-like spirals. The Veggetti has sharp stainless steel blades on each end, with one end producing thin spirals and the other end producing thick spirals. The spiralizer also comes with a closed food holder cap on one end which can be used to easily grip and feed the vegetable into the sharp stainless steel blades by simply pushing and turning it. Furthermore, the Veggetti spiralizer is easily grasped and works well for making spirals from vegetables instantly. No assembling is required for the Veggetti to work since all of its parts are completely pre-assembled.

HOW TO SPIRALIZE

Turning your vegetables into pasta with your Veggetti spiralizer is quite simple if you follow these 5 steps:

STEP 1: Ensure that your Veggetti is clean and ready for the spiralizing job.

STEP 2: Wash your vegetable and trim any undesired part. Reshape or resize your vegetable if necessary so that it fits into the Veggetti.

STEP 3: Position a plate to collect your vegetable spirals as you spiralize.

STEP 4: Firmly hold the middle of the Veggetti's metal handles and place the vegetable in either end of the spiralizer depending on whether you want thick or thin spirals.

STEP 5: Hold an end of your vegetable and push while turning it in a pencil-sharpening motion until you have enough spirals for your dish. Remember to use the food holder cap to hold the vegetable as it gets smaller or to prevent unnecessary slippage.

CARING TIPS

The Veggetti is safe for your dishwasher. You should wash the Veggetti spiralizer in warm soapy water or warm running water before each initial use. You should use a regular cleaning brush from your dishwasher or a new toothbrush to carefully clear the blades of any food residue. Always exercise extra care whenever you use the Veggetti as the blades are very sharp. The Veggetti is small enough for storing in a suitable kitchen drawer.

BEST VEGETABLES FOR VEGGETTI

The Veggetti works best with cylindrical-shaped and conical-shaped vegetables that are between approximately 4cm (1½") and 7cm (2¼") in diameter. The best vegetables to use are: squash, zucchini, potatoes, cucumbers, carrots and other similarly shaped veggies or fruits.

QUICK TIPS

Spiralizing vegetables using the Vegetti is easy. By using the Veggetti frequently, spiralized cooking will tend to become practically knowable. If you carefully follow the recipes in this cookbook, you should be able to always get flawless and pleasant results. Here are some tips to help you along your Veggetti spiralizing journey:

1. If your Veggetti didn't come with a separate cleaning brush, you should buy one. You will need a brush to easily remove vegetable residue from the blades or food holder cap of your spiralizer.

2. Sometimes you may need to go through your vegetable spirals with a kitchen scissors and quickly trim your spirals to a desired pasta size.

3. You should store your vegetable spaghetti and the sauce separately in order to avoid a runny and diluted sauce.

4. For more nutrient benefits, sometimes you can eat raw instead of cooked vegetable spirals.

5. For high water content vegetables such as cucumbers, you may need to use paper towels to gently pat dry any excess water seepage.

NOTE: *The information presented here is not by*

any means intended to be used in replacement of the manufacturer's instruction manual.

HOW TO SPIRALIZE DIFFERENT VEGETABLES

Generally, all vegetable spaghetti makers operate based on a similar principle. Of course, if you do not own a Veggetti, you may need to study your own spiralizer model and get fully acquainted with exactly how it works. Nevertheless, the following guidelines are intended to guide you into turning your favorite vegetables into spaghetti using the Veggetti.

ZUCCHINI, SUMMER SQUASH, YELLOW SQUASH

Wash your zucchini or squash then use a sharp knife to evenly chop off the nose end (the side opposite to the stem). Next, choose whether you will use the funnel end for thick spirals or thin spirals. Hold the stem of the zucchini or squash then push and turn it in a pencil-sharpening motion until you have enough spirals for your dish. Remember to use the food holder cap as your vegetable gets shorter and to prevent slippage.

CARROT, PARSNIP

Wash your carrot or parsnip then peel it with a vegetable peeler. Next, choose whether you will use the funnel end for thick spirals or thin spirals. Insert the larger end of the vegetable into the center of the funnel. Hold the smaller end (cone-shaped tip) of the vegetable as a handle while pushing and turning it in a pencil-sharpening motion until you have enough spirals for your dish.

CUCUMBER

Wash your cucumber then use a sharp knife to evenly chop off the nose end (the side opposite to the stem). If you decide to peel it, use the food holder cap to avoid any slippage accidents. Next, choose whether you will use the funnel end for thick spirals or thin spirals. Hold the stem of the cucumber then push and turn it in a pencil-sharpening motion until you have enough spirals for your dish.

SWEET POTATO, WHITE POTATO

Wash your potato then peel it with a vegetable peeler. Resize or reshape where needed if the potato is too large for the Veggetti. Next, choose whether you will use the funnel end for thick or thin spirals. Insert the potato into the center of the funnel. Use the Veggetti food holder cap to secure the potato then while pushing, turn it in a pencil-sharpening motion until you have enough spirals for your dish.

HOW TO USE THIS COOKBOOK

Though not all the recipes in this book are gluten-free, all recipes are low carb and are created to support a healthy lifestyle. After selecting a recipe, you should ensure that you have the ingredients and then follow the recipe's directions. Whenever a recipe lists a specific spiralized vegetable as an ingredient, you should use your Veggetti or other spiralizer model according to the manufacturer's instructions. If needed, you may also refer to the "How to Spiralize Different Vegetables" guidelines in this book. By referring to these guidelines, you should be able to make a good start. Moreover, for the sake of a hearty variety, this cookbook caters to two (2) recipe categories:

1. **LOW CARB RECIPES** – these recipes consist of a variety of vegetable spaghetti pasta noodles with an interesting combination of cheese or other healthy ingredients. Some of these recipes are gluten-free, but not all. This section is a perfect pick for those who are not on a gluten-free diet and still want to enjoy healthy and tasty low carb veggie pasta dishes.

2. **PALEO & GLUTEN-FREE RECIPES** – these recipes consist of a variety of vegetable spaghetti noodles combined with a variety of healthy gluten-free and dairy-free ingredients. This section is the perfect pick for those on a Paleo, gluten-free, dairy-free or low carb diet.

Overall, whichever category of recipe sparks your interest, you can rest assured that you are having a healthy low carb meal. Please feel free to make your own ingredient substitutions based on individual situations, preferences or diet.

Making Veggetti Spaghetti

With this hearty collection of easy and appetizing recipes, you will be able to cook a perfectly tasty Veggetti spaghetti meal every time. Furthermore, these recipes are particularly designed to help you maintain good health and even lose weight.

Now, it's time to start using your Veggetti to create healthy, easy and inspiring low carb meals.

Let's make Veggetti spaghetti!

6

LOW CARB BREAKFAST VEGGETTI RECIPES

Zucchini Kale Frittata

This is a delightfully enjoyable frittata for a great breakfast.
This lovely dish can be eaten for lunch also.

MAKES: 2 servings
PREPARATION TIME: 15 minutes
COOKING TIME: 20 minutes

---

3 Organic Eggs
2 Organic Egg Whites (or 2 more eggs)
1 Zucchini, spiralized and trimmed into 3-inch pieces
1 tablespoon Extra Virgin Olive Oil
2 Garlic Cloves, minced
2 cups Fresh Kale, trimmed and chopped
1 cup Cremini Mushrooms, sliced into ½-inch

thick pieces
Kosher Salt, to taste
Black Pepper, to taste

Directions

1. Preheat the oven to 350 degrees F. In a large bowl, beat together the egg whites, eggs and seasoning. Stir in the spiralized zucchini and set aside.
2. In a large oven proof skillet, heat the oil on a medium heat. Sauté the garlic for about 1 minute. Add the kale and mushrooms and cook for about 3 minutes. Stir in the egg mixture.
3. Transfer the skillet into the oven and bake for about 15 minutes.

Summer Squash Frittata

Enjoy this summer squash frittata which makes a pleasantly healthy and delicious meal. This wholesome summer squash dish is nicely combined with cheese and eggs.

MAKES: 4 servings
PREPARATION TIME: 10 minutes
COOKING TIME: 20 minutes

———————— ⌘ ————————

1 tablespoon Olive Oil
1 Garlic Clove, minced
4 Summer Squash, spiralized
3 Organic Eggs
6 Organic Egg Whites (or 3 more eggs)
Kosher Salt, to taste
Black Pepper, to taste
2 tablespoons low-fat or non-fat Milk
2 tablespoons Ricotta Cheese, crumbled

———————— ⌘ ————————

Directions

1. Preheat the oven to 350 degrees F. In an ovenproof skillet, heat oil over medium heat. After the oil is heated, add garlic

and allow to sauté for about half a minute. Add spiralized summer squash and cook while stirring occasionally for approximately 5 minutes. Take it from the heat.

2. In the meantime, in a bowl, add eggs, salt, black pepper and milk and beat well. Add egg mixture in skillet and combine thoroughly. Evenly sprinkle the ricotta cheese on top.

3. Allow to bake for 10 to 12 minutes or until eggs are set completely.

Cheesy Avocado Carrot Omelet

Enjoy one of the most delicious omelets with spiralized carrot, cheese and avocado. This nutritious omelet may soon become one of your breakfast favorites.

MAKES: 2 servings
PREPARATION TIME: 12 minutes
COOKING TIME: 10 minutes

2½ tablespoons Extra Virgin Olive Oil
2 medium Carrots, peeled and spiralized
5 large Organic Eggs
Kosher Salt, to taste
Black Pepper, to taste
2 tablespoons Gruyere Cheese, grated
2 slices (200g) Avocado, cubed
2 tablespoons Fresh Parsley, chopped

Directions

1. In a large non-stick skillet, heat a tablespoon of the oil on a medium heat. Add the spiralized carrot to the skillet and cook for 3 to 4 minutes

before carefully removing from the heat and setting aside.

2. In the meantime, in a bowl, add the eggs and seasoning, and beat well. In a large frying pan heat the remaining oil on a medium heat. Add the beaten eggs and use a wooden spoon to spread the eggs towards the edges of the frying pan. Cook for 1½ minutes. Place the carrots, grated gruyere cheese and avocado over the eggs. Carefully fold the omelet in half. Cook for a further 2 minutes.

3. Top with the chopped parsley and serve while still warm.

Breakfast Potato Jix

This is a healthy and delicious recipe for breakfast that is made with white potatoes. Enjoy this dish for breakfast or whenever you want.

MAKES: 4 servings
PREPARATION TIME: 15 minutes
COOKING TIME: 28-33 minutes

---

2 tablespoons Extra Virgin Olive Oil
1 White Potato, peeled and spiralized
1 Sweet Onion, chopped
2 Garlic Cloves, minced
12 Organic Eggs, cracked and set aside
Kosher Salt, to taste
Black Pepper, to taste
4 ounces Mozzarella Cheese, grated

Directions

1. Preheat the oven to 350 degrees F.
2. In an oven proof skillet, heat the oil on a medium heat. Add the spiralized white potato and sweet onion and

cook for about 8 minutes. Next, add the minced garlic and cook for another minute. Pour the cracked eggs over the sweet potato mixture. Sprinkle with salt, black pepper and mozzarella cheese.

3. Transfer the skillet into the oven and bake for 20 to 25 minutes.

Squash Bok Choy Frittata

This frittata uniquely combines summer squash with bok choy and eggs. The summer squash noodles add an interesting twist to this frittata.

MAKES: 4 servings
PREPARATION TIME: 12-15 minutes
COOKING TIME: 20 minutes

---

1 tablespoon Extra Virgin Coconut Oil
1 Garlic Clove, minced
3 Cups Fresh Bok Choy, trimmed and chopped
1 large Summer Squash, spiralized
Kosher Salt, to taste
Black Pepper, to taste
6 Organic Egg Whites, beaten
3 large Organic Eggs, beaten

Directions

1. Preheat the oven to 375 degrees F.
2. In an oven-proof skillet, heat the oil on a medium heat. Sauté the garlic for about 1 minute. Add the bok choi and

33

cook until the bok choi becomes wilted. Transfer half of the bok choy onto a plate. Place the spiralized summer squash over the bok choy. Place the remaining bok choy over the summer squash and sprinkle with salt and black pepper. Combine the beaten egg whites and whole eggs and spread the combined egg mixture over the bok choy and cook for a further 2 minutes.

3. Transfer the skillet into oven and bake for 15 to 18 minutes.

Cauliflower Chicken Medley

This is a really great dish for breakfast, lunch or dinner. The combination of eggs, chicken and cauliflower with spiralized zucchini creates a tasty dish.

MAKES: 2 servings
PREPARATION TIME: 20 minutes
COOKING TIME: 12-15 minutes

---

2 tablespoons Extra Virgin Olive Oil
2 large Organic Eggs
1 cup Cauliflower Florets
1 small White Onion, chopped
1 medium Yellow Bell Pepper, seeded and chopped
1 teaspoon Garlic, minced
1 teaspoon Fresh Ginger, minced
Kosher Salt, to taste
Black Pepper, to taste
1 teaspoon White Vinegar
3 tablespoons Soy Sauce
1 teaspoon Raw Sugar
1 skinless, boneless, Chicken Breast, cut into ½-inch strips

2 medium Zucchinis, spiralized

Directions

1. In a small skillet, heat 1 teaspoon of oil. Add the eggs and cook, whilst stirring, for 2 minutes. Remove the scrambled eggs from the pan and set to one side.

2. In a large skillet, heat the remaining oil on a medium heat. Add the cauliflower and cook for about 3 minutes. Add the onion, bell pepper, garlic and ginger and cook for 2 minutes. Season with salt and black pepper. Add the chicken and cook for about 2 minutes.

3. Meanwhile, in a bowl mix together the vinegar, soy sauce and sugar. Add in the scrambled eggs, spiralized zucchini and vinegar mixture and cook for 3 minutes. Serve as desired.

Yellow Squash Surprise

Enjoy an easy, tasty and nutritious dish with this recipe.
Even though this recipe has a relatively short cooking time,
you are assured that you are still having a healthy meal.

MAKES: 2 servings
PREPARATION TIME: 15 minutes
COOKING TIME: 10 minutes

---

2 tablespoons Extra Virgin Olive Oil
1 medium White Potato, peeled and spiralized
1 medium Yellow Squash, spiralized
4 Organic Eggs, cracked and placed in a bowl
2 tablespoons Gruyere Cheese, grated
Kosher Salt, to taste
Black Pepper, to taste

Directions

1. In a large skillet, heat 1 tablespoon of oil on a medium heat. Add the spiralized potato and cook for about 3 minutes. Next, add the spiralized

yellow squash and cook for 3 minutes.

2. Make a well in the center of the vegetables and pour the rest of the oil into the well. Pour the cracked the eggs into the well and sprinkle with grated cheese. Cover the skillet and cook for 2 to 3 minutes, or until the eggs are cooked to your satisfaction.

3. Sprinkle with salt and black pepper before serving.

Coodle Sandwich

This is a really quick and easily assembled spiralized carrot sandwich which makes a splendid and delicious addition to your breakfast menu.

MAKES: 2 servings
PREPARATION TIME: 15 minutes

---

1 medium Carrot, peeled, spiralized and trimmed into 2-inch pieces
2 tablespoons Black Olives, pitted and sliced
3 tablespoons chopped Cabbage
4 Tomato Slices, chopped
½ cup Baby Spinach, torn
½ cup Gruyere Cheese, grated
¼ cup Garlic Hummus
2 large Iceberg Lettuce Leaves

Directions

1. In a large bowl, mix together all of the ingredients, except for the hummus and lettuce.
2. Spoon the vegetable mixture evenly

into the lettuce leaves.
3. Roll the leaves and serve.

Breakfast Squash Casserole

This is an easy way to prepare a tasty and healthy breakfast casserole from summer squash.

MAKES: 4 servings
PREPARATION TIME: 20 minutes
COOKING TIME: 50 minutes

---

4 Large Organic Eggs
2 tablespoons Coconut Milk
1 tablespoon Extra Virgin Coconut Oil
¼ cup Almond Meal, divided
Kosher Salt, to taste
Black Pepper, to taste
4 cups Summer Squash, spiralized
1 tablespoon finely chopped Scallion

Directions

1. Preheat oven to 300 degrees F. Prepare an 8x8-inch baking dish with oil or cooking spray.
2. In a large bowl, add the following ingredients: eggs, coconut milk,

coconut oil, 3 tablespoons of almond meal, kosher salt and black pepper. Beat all ingredients together until well combined. Stir in spiralized summer squash. Place a third part (1/3) of squash noodles into prepared baking dish. Place a third part (1/3) of scallion over noodles. Repeat this layers routine twice. Transfer the remaining egg mixture from bowl over the squash layers. Sprinkle evenly with the remaining almond meal.

3. Allow to bake for 45-50 minutes or until completely.

Potato Egg Deli

This is an amazing and tasty way to make use of your Veggetti spiralizer. Enjoy this easy baked potato dish which makes a healthy meal for everyone.

MAKES: 3-4 servings
PREPARATION TIME: 15 minutes
COOKING TIME: 33 minutes

---

2 Sweet Potatoes, peeled and spiralized
5 tablespoons Extra Virgin Olive Oil
1 teaspoon Cayenne Pepper
Kosher Salt, to taste
Black Pepper, to taste
8 large Organic Eggs, cracked and placed in a bowl

Directions

1. Preheat the oven to 400 degrees F. Grease 2 baking sheets.
2. Arrange the spiralized potatoes on the prepared baking sheets. Drizzle with 2 tablespoons of oil and sprinkle with

spices. Bake for about 30 minutes, flipping once after 15 minutes.

3. In the meantime, in a large frying pan heat the remaining oil on a low heat. Pour the cracked eggs into the frying pan. Use a metal or wooden spoon to pour the hot oil over whites until set and then spoon the oil over the yolks while leaving the yolks runny. Cook for about 3 minutes. Top the potato with the fried eggs and serve immediately.

Squashy Egg Dish

*Want one of those quick fix breakfasts? This is a good pick.
Enjoy this easy and tasty recipe for a satisfying breakfast.*

MAKES: 2 servings
PREPARATION TIME: 15 minutes
COOKING TIME: 4 minutes

---

*1 medium Yellow Squash, spiralized
Kosher Salt, to taste
Black Pepper, to taste
1½ tablespoons Extra Virgin Olive Oil
1 tablespoon Soy Sauce
4 Organic Eggs
1 tablespoon fresh Scallion, chopped
1 ounce Gruyere Cheese, grated*

Directions

1. In a large frying pan, heat the remaining oil on a low heat. Carefully crack the eggs into the frying pan. Use a metal or wooden spoon to pour the hot oil over whites until set and then

spoon the oil over the yolks while leaving the yolks runny. Cook for about 3 minutes.

2. In the meantime, place the spiralized yellow squash in a microwave safe dish or bowl. Sprinkle with salt and black pepper. Microwave on high for about 1 minute. Drizzle with ½ tablespoon of oil and soy sauce. Microwave for 1 extra minute. Transfer the yellow squash to a serving plate.

3. Top the yellow squash with the fried eggs, scallion and cheese. Serve as desired.

Special Zucchini Patties

Use your spiralized zucchini to make this tasty egg dish for breakfast. These zucchini patties can be a great hit for a holiday breakfast as well.

MAKES: 4 servings
PREPARATION TIME: 20 minutes
COOKING TIME: 40 minutes

---

2 Large Organic Eggs
¼ teaspoon Ground Cumin
½ teaspoon Red Pepper Flakes, crushed
Kosher Salt to taste
Black Pepper, to taste
¼ cup Butter, melted
2 tablespoons Almond Meal
2 medium Zucchinis, spiralized and chopped

Directions

1. Preheat the oven to 375 degrees F. Prepare 2 baking sheets by lining them with greased parchment papers.
2. In a large bowl, add eggs and spices and beat well. Add butter and flour and

3. mix until well combined. Add remaining ingredients and mix thoroughly. Take about ½ cup of the egg mixture and place it into prepared baking sheet and shape it like a patty. Repeat with the rest of the mixture and arrange in both baking sheets in a single row.

4. Allow to bake for 10 minutes. Reduce the heat temperature of the oven to 350 degrees F. Bake for an additional 15 minutes. Carefully flip the patties and bake for 15 more minutes. Serve as desired.

LOW CARB LUNCH & DINNER VEGGETTI RECIPES

Mushroom Zoodle Salad

Enjoy this very bright salad which makes an ultimate light meal or side dish. This dish has a nicely spiced vinaigrette and is perfect for a light and nutritious lunch.

MAKES: 2 servings
PREPARATION TIME: 15-18 minutes

Salad Ingredients
⅓ cup Fresh Mushrooms, sliced
1 medium Zucchini, spiralized
⅓ cup Yellow Bell Pepper, seeded and sliced
⅓ cup Celery, sliced
⅓ cup Sweet Onion, sliced
1 small Tomato, sliced
⅓ cup Fresh Basil, chopped

Vinaigrette Ingredients
2 tablespoons Red Wine Vinegar
2 tablespoons Olive Oil
1 small Garlic Clove, minced
¼ teaspoon Dried Thyme, crushed
Kosher Salt, to taste

Directions0

1. In a large serving bowl, gently combine all the vegetables together
2. In a smaller bowl, add all the vinaigrette ingredients and beat until well combined.
3. Pour the vinaigrette over the salad, gently toss to coat well, and serve immediately.

Veggie Shrimp Stir-Fry

Enjoy this flavorful and healthy shrimp stir-fry recipe for lunch or even a light dinner. Garnish with fresh parsley leaves and enjoy.

MAKES: 2 servings
PREPARATION TIME: 15-18 minutes
COOKING TIME: 10 minutes

1½ tablespoons Olive Oil
1 Garlic Clove, minced
2 tablespoons Scallions, chopped
1 cup Mushrooms, sliced
1 tablespoon Soy Sauce
1 medium Carrot, peeled and spiralized
8-ounces Shrimp, peeled and deveined
Kosher Salt, to taste
Black Pepper, to taste

Directions

1. In a large non-stick skillet, heat the oil on a medium heat. Sauté the garlic for 1 minute. Add the soy sauce and all

vegetables the vegetables EXCEPT the carrot and stir fry for 5 minutes.
2. Add the carrot and shrimp and cook for 3 to 4 minutes.
3. Season with salt and black pepper before serving.

Cucumber Garden Salad

This is a colorful and uplifting garden salad. It is quite tasty and it is prepared using garden-fresh green vegetables. Garnish with freshly grated lime zest before serving and enjoy.

MAKES: 2 servings
PREPARATION TIME: 15-18 minutes

Salad Ingredients

1 cup Mixed Salad Leaves (Butter head, Endive, Iceberg etc.), chopped
1 cup Baby Spinach Leaves
½ Avocado, peeled, pitted and sliced thinly
1 Green Bell pepper, seeded and sliced thinly
1 medium Cucumber, spiralized

Vinaigrette Ingredients

1 tablespoon Balsamic Vinegar
2 tablespoons Olive Oil
1 small Garlic Clove, minced
Kosher Salt, to taste

Directions

1. In a large serving bowl, mix together all the salad ingredients.
2. In a smaller bowl, combine all of the vinaigrette ingredients and combine well.
3. Pour the vinaigrette over the salad, toss gently to coat well and serve immediately.

Cod & Vegetables Stew

This unbelievably easy and tasty recipe is perfect for a quick lunch or even dinner. Sprinkle a little fresh lemon juice over the finished dish and enjoy.

MAKES: 2 servings
PREPARATION TIME: 15 minutes
COOKING TIME: 15 minutes

---

1 tablespoon Extra Virgin Olive Oil
1 cup Onion, chopped
2 small Garlic Cloves, minced
½ cup Celery, sliced
2 cups Fish Broth
1 cup Tomatoes, chopped finely
½ pound Cod, cut into bite size pieces
1 medium Carrot, peeled and spiralized
¼ cup Fresh Parsley, chopped
Kosher Salt, to taste
Black Pepper, to taste

Directions

1. In a large skillet, heat the oil on a

medium heat. Sauté the onion, garlic and celery for 4 to 5 minutes. Add the tomatoes and fish broth and then bring to boiling point.

2. Reduce the heat and simmer for 4 to 5 minutes.

3. Add the fish, carrot and parsley, and cook for 4-5 more minutes.

4. Season with black pepper and salt before serving hot.

Tangy Beef Steak

This is a quick and easy steak recipe with balsamic flavored tomatoes and parsnips. It may be served with a garnishing of fresh parsley.

MAKES: 2 servings
PREPARATION TIME: 10 minutes
COOKING TIME: 12 minutes

½ cup Balsamic Vinegar
⅓ cup Roma Tomatoes, seeded and chopped
1 medium Parsnip, peeled and spiralized
2 teaspoons Extra Virgin Olive Oil
2 (4-ounces) Grass-Fed Lean Beef Tenderloin Steaks
Kosher Salt, to taste
Black Pepper, to taste

Directions

1. Add the balsamic vinegar to a small sauce pan and bring to the boil on a medium heat. Reduce the heat to low and simmer for about 4 minutes. Stir

in the tomatoes and parsnip and simmer for another minute then remove from the heat.

2. In the meantime, in a skillet, heat the oil on a medium-high heat. Add the steak and sprinkle with salt and black pepper. Cook for about 5 minutes per side.

3. Place the steaks onto a serving plate and top with the tomato and parsnip mixture before serving.

Rich Nutty Egg Salad

This is a light and crunchy salad with healthy protein, fiber and other essential nutrients. Enjoy this salad for a healthy lunch or maybe even dinner.

MAKES: 4 servings
PREPARATION TIME: 10 minutes

---

8 Organic Eggs, hard boiled and chopped
1 medium Cucumber, spiralized
½ cup Cabbage, chopped
I medium Carrot, peeled and spiralized
2 tablespoons Scallions, sliced thinly
¼ cup non-fat Plain Yogurt
Kosher Salt, to taste
¼ cup chopped Pecans

Directions

1. In a large serving bowl, add eggs and vegetables and gently mix to combine.
2. In another bowl, add yogurt, salt and mix well.
3. Add yogurt mixture into vegetables

and gently mix.

4. Top this salad with chopped pecan nuts. Serve immediately.

Cheesy Squash Cake

This delightful summer squash dish is splendid in flavor. This is another great way that you can hide your spiralized veggies into a delicious dish.

MAKES: 4 servings
PREPARATION TIME: 10 minutes
COOKING TIME: 20 minutes

2-3 medium (about 453g) Summer Squash, spiralized
½ cup Mozzarella Cheese, grated freshly
1 tablespoon fresh Basil, chopped
2/3 cup Onion, chopped finely
1 large Organic Egg, beaten
Kosher salt and Black Pepper, to taste
1 tablespoon Extra-virgin Coconut Oil or Olive Oil

Directions

1. Preheat the oven to 400 degrees F. Lightly, grease a baking pan.
2. In a large bowl, add spiralized summer

squash and cheese and mix together.

3. In another bowl, add remaining ingredients except oil and mix well.
4. Mix cheese mixture into egg mixture.
5. In a non-stick pan, heat oil on medium heat. Fill 1/3 of a cup with mixture and place in the pan. Slightly, press down to make a 3-inch sized cake.
6. Cook for about 3 to 4 minutes or until golden brown. Repeat with the remaining mixture.
7. Transfer the cakes into prepared baking pan.
8. Bake for about 10 minutes. Serve this summer squash cake with avocado slices or as desired.

Coodle Zoodle Salad

The spiralized carrot and zucchini of this salad are really great beauty enhancers. Also, the combination of flavors from the vegetables and the dressing makes an irresistible lunch salad.

MAKES: 2 servings
PREPARATION TIME: 15-18 minutes

Salad Ingredients

¼ cup Green Cabbage, shredded
¼ cup Purple Cabbage, shredded
¼ cup Bean Sprouts
1 small Carrot, spiralized
1 small Zucchini, spiralized
1 tablespoon Scallion, chopped

Dressing Ingredients

1 small Garlic Clove, minced
¼ small Jalapeño, seeded and copped
1 tablespoon Fresh Cilantro, chopped
1 tablespoon Fresh Lime juice
½ teaspoon Soy Sauce
1 teaspoon Water

Kosher Salt, to taste

Directions

1. In a large serving bowl mix together all of the salad ingredients.
2. In a blender, add all of the dressing ingredients and blend until well combined.
3. Pour the dressing over the salad and toss to coat well.

Stir-Fry Veggie Combo

This stir-fry vegetable recipe makes a pleasingly delicious meatless stir-fry lunch dish. This recipe is a good way to enjoy the delicate taste of spiralized carrots and bok choy.

MAKES: 4 servings
PREPARATION TIME: 10 minutes
COOKING TIME: 10 minutes

1½ tablespoons Extra-virgin Coconut Oil
2 Garlic Cloves, minced
4 Scallions, chopped
1 Red Bell Pepper, seeded and diced
1 Yellow Bell Pepper, seeded and diced
1 medium Carrot, spiralized
1 pound (453 grams) Baby Bok Choy,
trimmed and torn
Kosher Salt to taste

Directions

1. In a large pan, heat oil on medium-high heat.
2. Add garlic and sauté for 1 minute.

3. Add scallions and bell peppers and cook, stirring often for about 2 to 3 minutes.
4. Add carrot and bok choy and cook for 4 minutes or until bok choy is wilted.
5. Serve as desired.

Chicken Zoodle Soup

This is a great idea for a tasty and hearty soup. Enjoy this recipe which as another creative way to use your Veggetti and eat your vegetables.

MAKES: 4 servings
PREPARATION TIME: 15 minutes
COOKING TIME: 35-40 minutes

---

2 tablespoons Extra Virgin Olive Oil
1 medium White Onion, chopped
3 Garlic Cloves, minced
2 cups Celery, chopped
2 medium Carrots, peeled and spiralized
7-8 cups Chicken Broth
3 medium Zucchinis, spiralized
2 Grass-Fed cooked, skinless, boneless, shredded Chicken Breasts
Kosher Salt, to taste
Black Pepper, to taste

Directions

1. In a large soup pan, heat the oil on a

medium heat. Sauté the onion for 4 minutes before sautéing the garlic for 1 minute. Add the celery and cook for another 4 minutes.

2. Add the broth and bring the mixture to boil. Reduce the heat, cover and simmer for 20 to 25 minutes. Stir in the spiralized carrots, zucchini and shredded chicken, and cook for 3 minutes more.

3. Season with salt and pepper, remove from the heat and serve hot.

Grilled Chicken Zoodles

This simple zucchini pasta dish is rich in flavors and delicious, and may surely become one of your favorite dishes.

MAKES: 4 servings
PREPARATION TIME: 10 minutes
COOKING TIME: 20 minutes

---

2 medium (about 453 grams) Zucchinis, spiralized
2 boneless, skinless Chicken Breast Fillets
Kosher Salt, to taste
Black Pepper, to taste
1 teaspoon Dried Oregano, crushed
2 tablespoons Extra Virgin Olive Oil
3 Garlic Cloves, chopped
2 teaspoons crushed Red Pepper Flakes
1 teaspoon Fresh Lime or Lemon Juice
3 tablespoons Gruyere Cheese, grated
2 tablespoons Fresh Basil, chopped

Directions

1. Heat the grill to a medium-high heat.

Sprinkle the chicken with the kosher salt, black pepper and oregano. Grill for about 5 minutes per side. Remove from the grill and slice the chicken as evenly as possible.

2. In a skillet, heat the oil on medium heat. Add the red pepper flakes, garlic, spiralized zucchini and sauté for about 2 minutes. Remove from the heat. Transfer the zucchini into a large serving bowl. Stir in the cooked chicken and lime or lemon juice. Season with kosher salt and black pepper. Top with cheese. Garnish with basil and serve.

Crabmeat Squash Bowl

This recipe has an Italian flavor and is an enjoyable way to combine freshly spiralized yellow squash and ripe tomatoes with crabmeat.

MAKES: 4 servings
PREPARATION TIME: 10 minutes
COOKING TIME: 30 minutes

1½ cups Yellow Squash, spiralized
3 tablespoons Extra Virgin Olive Oil
2 Garlic Cloves, minced
½ cup Chicken Broth
2 cups Roma Tomatoes, chopped
Kosher Salt, to taste
Black Pepper, to taste
1 tablespoon Butter
1 pound (about 453g) Crabmeat
1 teaspoon Italian Seasoning

Directions
1. In a saucepan heat 2 tablespoons of oil on a medium heat. Add the garlic and

saunté for about 2 minutes. Add the tomatoes and broth. Reduce the heat to medium-low. Simmer and stir occasionally for 20 minutes. Stir in the kosher salt, black pepper and butter.

2. Season the crabmeat with the Italian seasoning. In a large skillet heat the remaining oil on medium-high heat. Add the crabmeat and cook for about 2 minutes. Next, add the spiralized yellow squash and allow it to cook for another 3 minutes. Carefully combine the crabmeat and yellow squash with the chopped tomato mixture. Sprinkle with salt if needed and transfer to a serving bowl.

Herbed Lamb Pasta

Enjoy this dish of fresh herb flavors with lamb on your table.
Savor the interesting flavors by chewing slowly.

MAKES: 4 servings
PREPARATION TIME: 10 minutes
COOKING TIME: 10 minutes

1½ cups Zucchini, spiralized
2 tablespoons Olive Oil
1½ pounds Lean Ground Lamb
2 cups Grape Tomatoes
3 Garlic Cloves, finely chopped
1 large Shallot, chopped
Kosher Salt, to taste
¼ cup Vegetable Broth
¼ cup Fresh Basil, chopped
¼ cup Fresh Thyme, chopped

Directions

1. In a skillet heat the oil on medium-high heat. Add the lamb and cook for about 5 minutes, or until brown. Add the

tomatoes and cook for 4 minutes. Add the garlic, shallot, kosher salt and black pepper, and cook for a further 2 minutes. Add the spiralized zucchini and cook for another 2 minutes.

2. Add the vegetable broth and fresh herbs. Gently combine well and serve.

Zucchini Kale Soup

This is a satisfying and appetizing soup. This dish will be ideal for cold weather or whenever you want a nice soup for dinner.

MAKES: 2 servings
PREPARATION TIME: 10 minutes
COOKING TIME: 15 minutes

---

1 tablespoon Extra Virgin Olive Oil
1 teaspoon Garlic, minced
1 tablespoon Fresh Ginger, minced
3½ cups Homemade Vegetable Broth
2 tablespoons Soy Sauce
1 teaspoon White Vinegar
1 cup Kale, trimmed and chopped
2 organic Eggs, beaten
1 Zucchini, spiralized
2 tablespoons Scallion, chopped
2 tablespoons Celery, chopped
Kosher Salt, to taste
Freshly Ground Black Pepper, to taste

Directions

1. In a large soup pan, heat the oil on a medium heat. Sauté the garlic and ginger for about 1 minute. Add the broth, soy sauce and vinegar, and bring to the boil. Cook for about 4 to 5 minutes. Add the kale and cook for a further 4 to 5 minutes.

2. Slowly, add the beaten eggs, stirring continuously. Stir in the zucchini, scallion and seasoning. Cook for 3 to 4 minutes before serving hot.

Beef & Kale Pasta Mix

*This spiralized pasta recipe of beef, kale, potato and spices
delivers a pleasing blend of flavors.*

MAKES: 4 servings
PREPARATION TIME: 10 minutes
COOKING TIME: 18 minutes

---

*½ pound (226g) Ground Lean Beef
3 Garlic Cloves, finely chopped
1 Onion, finely chopped
1½ cups Beef Broth
1½ cups canned Tomatoes with juice
1 teaspoon Fresh Basil, chopped
Kosher Salt, to taste
Black Pepper, to taste
1 White Potato, spiralized
1¼ cups Kale, trimmed and chopped*

Directions

1. In a large non-stick skillet heat the oil
on a medium-high heat. Add the beef
and cook for about 5 minutes. Add the

garlic and onion, and cook for 5 minutes.

2. Add the broth, tomatoes with juice, basil, kosher salt and black pepper. Bring to a boil, then reduce the heat to medium-low while continuing to cook for a further 3 minutes. Add the spiralized potatoes, cover with a lid and continue cooking for another 5 minutes or until the potato is cooked (do not overcook).

3. Add the kale and cook for a further 2 to 3 minutes. Serve.

Tangy Carrot Salad

This is one of the easiest salads to prepare, being light, crunchy and delightfully tasty.

MAKES: 2-3 servings
PREPARATION TIME: 10 minutes

---

2 medium Carrots, peeled and spiralized
1 Garlic Clove, finely minced
2 tablespoons Fresh Lime or Lemon juice
2 tablespoons Extra Virgin Olive Oil
2 tablespoons Scallions (white part), finely chopped
½ tablespoon Fresh Basil, chopped
½ tablespoon Fresh Cilantro, chopped
Kosher Salt, to taste

Directions

1. In a large bowl combine all the ingredients and toss together. Refrigerate to chill before serving.

Veggie Medley Fish

Enjoy this delightfully delicious and colorful combination of tilapia fillets, vegetables and herbs.

MAKES: 4 servings
PREPARATION TIME: 10 minutes
COOKING TIME: 13 minutes

---

1 tablespoon Extra Virgin Olive Oil, separated
4 Tilapia Fillets
Kosher Salt, to taste
Black Pepper, to taste
1 medium Carrot, peeled and spiralized
1 medium Zucchini, spiralized
1 Summer Squash, spiralized
¾ cup Fennel Stalks, julienned or cut into fine strips
1 cup Red Onion, sliced
3 Garlic Cloves, minced
¼ cup Fresh Thyme, chopped
½ tablespoon Balsamic Vinegar
½ teaspoon Dried Oregano, crushed

Directions

1. In a large nonstick skillet, heat 1 teaspoon oil on medium-high heat. Add fish and sprinkle with kosher salt and black pepper. Cook for about 4 minutes per side. Transfer into a plate and cover with foil paper to keep it warm.
2. In a large bowl, add remaining ingredients and mix together. In the same skillet, heat remaining oil. Add the vegetable mixture. Season with kosher salt and black pepper. Sauté for about 4 to 5 minutes.
3. In a serving plate, arrange vegetable mixture beside the fish and serve.

Minty Cheese Zoodles

This is a very easy spiralized zucchini dish which serves up a nutritious and tasty vegetable dish. You can serve this with your favorite protein or you can serve it by itself. For even more variation, you may add ½ cup to toasted pecan or walnuts as another topping ingredient as you serve this dish.

MAKES: 2 servings
PREPARATION TIME: 20 minutes
COOKING TIME: 5 minutes

½ tablespoon Extra Virgin Olive Oil
1 cup Scallions, sliced
2 medium Zucchinis, spiralized
Kosher Salt, to taste
Black Pepper, to taste
½ tablespoon Dried Thyme, crushed
2 tablespoons Feta Cheese, crumbled
1 teaspoon Fresh Mint Leaves, finely minced

Directions

1. In a nonstick skillet, heat oil on medium heat. Add scallions and zucchini and sauté for about 5 minutes.

2. Season with kosher salt, black pepper and thyme. While serving, top with feta cheese and mint.

Sweet & Sour Carrots

This is another quick and easy way to have your spiralized carrots. Enjoy this dish with dinner or lunch.

MAKES: 2-3 servings
PREPARATION TIME: 5 minutes
COOKING TIME: 13 minutes

---

3 medium Carrots, spiralized
Kosher Salt, to taste
2 tablespoons Butter
2 tablespoons Honey
¼ cup Fresh Orange Juice
1½ tablespoon Balsamic Vinegar
4 Scallions, chopped finely
1 teaspoon Cornstarch
1 tablespoon Fresh Basil, chopped

Directions

1. Place carrots and kosher salt in a water-filled saucepan. Boil for about 8 minutes. Drain well.
2. In the same saucepan or a new pan,

add remaining ingredients except basil. Cook for about 3 minutes. Gently stir in boiled carrots and basil and cook for 2 minutes. Serve.

Zesty Collard Greens

This salad recipe uses collard greens to make an excellent salad along with the zucchini and olives. Enjoy this quick and easy meal for dinner or lunch.

MAKES: 2 servings
PREPARATION TIME: 10 minutes
COOKING TIME: 15 minutes

---

1 medium Zucchini, spiralized
2 tablespoons Extra Virgin Olive Oil
1 Garlic Clove, minced
1 bunch Collard Greens, chopped
1 teaspoon Fresh Lime or Lemon Juice
2 teaspoons Green Olives, pitted and chopped
Kosher Salt, to taste
¼ cup Gruyere Cheese, grated

Directions

1. In a skillet, heat the oil on a medium heat. Add the garlic and sauté for a minute. Add the collard greens and zucchini and cook for 4 minutes, gently

86

stirring occasionally. Stir in the lime or lemon juice, olives and kosher salt. Top with the cheese and serve.

Tomato Sautéed Chicken

This is a simple and satisfying chicken recipe which combines parsnip and tomatoes to make a filling dish. The parsnip in this recipe can be substituted with carrot if you prefer.

MAKES: 4 servings
PREPARATION TIME: 10 minutes
COOKING TIME: 30 minutes

———————— ⌘ ————————

2½ teaspoons Extra Virgin Olive Oil
4 boneless, skinless Chicken Breasts, halved by slicing
3 tablespoons Onion, chopped
2 Garlic Cloves, minced
2½ cups Plum Tomatoes, chopped
¼ cup Balsamic Vinegar
¾ tablespoon Fresh Oregano, chopped
1 teaspoon Fresh Thyme, chopped
1 medium Parsnip, peeled and spiralized
6 tablespoons Black Olives, pitted and halved
Kosher Salt, to taste
Black Pepper, to taste
3 tablespoons Fresh Tarragon, chopped

———————— ⌘ ————————

Directions

1. In a large skillet heat 1½ teaspoons of the oil on a medium heat. Add the chicken breasts and cook for 4 to 5 minutes per side. Set aside the chicken on a plate.

2. In the same skillet heat the remaining oil. Add the onion and sauté for 3 to 4 minutes. Add the garlic and tomatoes and sauté for a further minute.

3. Reduce the heat to low. Add the vinegar and simmer for 5 minutes. Stir in the oregano and thyme, and simmer for a further 5 minutes.

4. Return the chicken to the skillet and add in the spiralized parsley. Cover, and cook for approximately 6 minutes, or until the chicken is cooked. Stir in the olives, kosher salt, black pepper and tarragon, and cook for a further 1 minute. Serve warm.

Zucchini Grilled Fish

*This is a tangy flavored quick and easy grilled fish recipe
that is nicely combined with zucchini and feta cheese.*

MAKES: 4 servings
PREPARATION TIME: 10 minutes
COOKING TIME: 10 minutes

---

2 Cod Fillets
1 tablespoon Extra Virgin Olive Oil
¼ teaspoon Dried Dill, crushed
¼ teaspoon Dried Rosemary, crushed
Kosher Salt, to taste
Black Pepper, to taste
2 Zucchinis, spiralized
3 tablespoons Green Olives, pitted and sliced
¼ cup Red Bell Pepper, seeded and chopped
2 cups Fresh Kale, trimmed and torn
¼ cup Scallions, chopped
3 tablespoons Fresh Lemon Juice
2 tablespoons Feta Cheese, crumbled

Directions

1. Preheat the grill. Place the fish fillets

on the grill pan. Coat with the olive oil, dill, rosemary, kosher salt and black pepper. Grill for about 10 minutes. Set aside to cool for 5 minutes then cut into bite size pieces.

2. In a large serving bowl combine together the fish, spiralized zucchini and remaining ingredients, except for the cheese. Toss to coat well.

3. Top with the feta cheese and serve.

Grilled Beef Salad

This is a tasty grilled beef recipe with a healthy salad mix.
You may have this satisfying beef salad at lunch or dinner.
Garnish this dish with fresh parsley leaves.

MAKES: 2 servings
PREPARATION TIME: 20 minutes
COOKING TIME: 12 minutes

Salad Ingredients
2 teaspoons Extra Virgin Olive Oil
½ pound (226g) Grass Fed Beef Steak
Kosher Salt, to taste
Black Pepper, to taste
1 cup Bean Sprouts
2 cups Grape Tomatoes, halved
1 medium Cucumber, spiralized
1 Red Onion, sliced thinly
1 cup Fresh Lettuce Leaves, torn
½ Bunch Coriander Leaves, chopped
½ Bunch Basil Leaves, chopped

Vinaigrette Ingredients
1 Garlic Clove, minced
1 teaspoon Extra Virgin Olive Oil

1 teaspoon Balsamic Vinegar
1 teaspoon Fresh Lime Juice
1 teaspoon Lime Zest, grated freshly
Kosher Salt, to taste
Black Pepper, to taste

Directions

1. Preheat the grill to medium. Grease the grill grate.
2. Sprinkle steak with salt and black pepper. Grill for about 6 minutes on each side. Transfer aside to cool slightly. Slice the steak thinly crosswise.
3. In the meantime, in a small bowl, add garlic, oil, vinegar, lime juice, zest, salt and black pepper and beat until well combined.
4. In a large serving bowl, add beef and remaining ingredients. Pour dressing and toss to coat well. Serve immediately.

Baked Spicy Meatballs

This is a pleasing recipe for a simple or over-the-top family dinner. The blend of spices, beef and vegetables adds tasty flavors.

MAKES: 2 servings
PREPARATION TIME: 20 minutes
COOKING TIME: 40 minutes

½ tablespoon Ground Coriander
½ tablespoon Ground Cumin, divided
1 teaspoon Cayenne Pepper, divided
1 teaspoon Smoked Paprika, divided
Kosher Salt, to taste
Black Pepper, to taste
1 tablespoon Olive Oil
1 Garlic Clove, minced
1 Red Onion, shredded
2 tablespoons Fresh Scallion Leaves, minced
2 small Zucchinis, spiralized
1 cup Tomatoes, chopped finely
½ pound Grass-Fed Lean Ground Beef

Directions

1. Preheat the oven to 350 degrees F. In a bowl, mix together all of the spices. Leave aside.
2. In a large ovenproof skillet, heat the oil on a medium heat. Sauté the garlic for 1 minute. Add the onion, scallion leaves and zucchini, and sauté for 4 to 5 minutes. Add half of the prepared spice mixture and sauté for a further minute. Add the tomatoes and cook for about 4 minutes before removing the skillet from the heat.
3. Meanwhile, in a bowl, mix together the beef and remaining spice mixture. Make your desired size balls from the beef mixture. Place the meatballs into the skillet and gently press them into the vegetable mixture.
4. Place the skillet in the oven and bake for 25 to 30 minutes.

PALEO, GLUTEN-FREE & DAIRY-FREE RECIPES

Carrot Stewed Shrimp

This dish makes a delicious shrimp stew that gets a yellow and green backdrop from the spiralized carrots and fresh parsley. Enjoy this hearty and flavorsome dish for lunch or dinner.

MAKES: 4 servings
PREPARATION TIME: 15 minutes
COOKING TIME: 50 minutes

---

1 cup Fresh Tomatoes, crushed
4 cups Homemade Fish Broth
2 tablespoons organic Extra Virgin Coconut Oil
¼ teaspoon Cayenne Pepper
4 Carrots, peeled and spiralized
1 pound (453g) large Shrimp, peeled and deveined

½ cup Fresh Parsley, chopped
1 tablespoon Fresh Lime juice
Sea Salt, to taste
Freshly Ground Black Pepper, to taste

Directions

1. In a large saucepan, add the tomatoes, broth, oil and cayenne pepper and bring to a boil on a high heat. Reduce the heat to medium-low. Cover tightly and cook for 35 to 45 minutes.
2. Uncover and stir in the carrots and shrimp. Cook for a further 5 minutes. Stir in the parsley, lime juice, salt and black pepper and serve.

Asparagus Steamed Fish

This tilapia fillet is nicely prepared in a quick and easy way. It is nicely combined with vegetables and makes a graceful dinner.

MAKES: 2 servings
PREPARATION TIME: 15 minutes
COOKING TIME: 5 minutes

---

2 bunches Fresh Asparagus, trimmed
2 Tilapia Fish Fillets
2 tablespoons Scallions, thinly chopped
2 small Carrots, peeled and spiralized
2 Garlic Cloves, minced
1 teaspoon Fresh Ginger, minced
1 tablespoon Fresh Lemon juice
1 tablespoon Coconut Vinegar
¼ teaspoon Chilli powder
Sea Salt, to taste
Freshly Ground Black Pepper, to taste

Directions

1. Arrange a large sheet of baking paper on a smooth surface and place the fish

fillets on the baking paper. Top with the vegetables, except for the asparagus, and drizzle with the lemon juice and vinegar. Sprinkle with the spices. Fold the baking paper to seal the packet around fish and vegetables.

2. Place the asparagus into a bamboo steamer basket and arrange the fish packet over the asparagus.

3. In a large pan, add 1-inch of water and bring to the boil. Set the steamer basket into the pan of boiling water and steam, covered, for about 5 minutes.

Garden Fresh Wraps

These lettuce wraps are excitingly tasty. They deliver a light low carb meal and garden fresh veggie flavors.

MAKES: 2 servings
PREPARATION TIME: 20 minutes

---

1 cup cooked boneless grass-fed Chicken Breast, chopped
1 Cucumber, spiralized and trimmed into 1½-pieces
¼ cup Tomatoes, seeded and sliced thinly
¼ cup Red Onion, sliced thinly
2 tablespoons finely diced Fresh Cilantro Leaves
1 teaspoon Coconut Vinegar
Sea Salt, to taste
2 large Iceberg Lettuce Leaves

Directions

1. In a large bowl, except for the lettuce, mix together all of the ingredients.

2. Spoon the chicken and vegetable mixture evenly into the lettuce leaves.
3. Roll the leaves and serve.

Zucchini Beef Soup

This soup makes use of pre-cooked ground beef and offers a warming and soothing meal for dinner or during the winter.

MAKES: 2 servings
PREPARATION TIME: 20 minutes
COOKING TIME: 17 minutes

---

1 tablespoon Extra Virgin Coconut Oil
1 Sweet Onion, chopped
2 cups Yellow Bell Pepper, seeded and sliced thinly
2 teaspoons Dried Thyme, crushed
1 teaspoon Dried Oregano, crushed
½ teaspoon Cayenne Pepper
1½ cup Fresh Tomatoes, finely chopped
3 cups Homemade Beef Broth
2½ cups Organic Coconut Milk
1 cup Homemade Pumpkin Puree
2 cups cooked Ground Beef
2 Zucchinis, spiralized
3½ cups Fresh Kale, trimmed and chopped
Sea Salt, to taste
Freshly Ground Black Pepper, to taste

3 tablespoons minced Parsley Leaves

Directions

1. In a soup pan, heat the oil on a medium heat. Sauté the onion and bell pepper for about 5 minutes. Add the herbs along with the cayenne pepper and sauté for 1 minute more. Add the chopped tomatoes and cook for another 4 minutes.
2. Add the homemade beef broth and bring to a boil. Reduce the heat, stir in coconut milk and homemade pumpkin puree. Simmer for about 2 minutes. Stir in the cooked ground beef, zucchini and kale and cook for a further 5 minutes.
3. Season with black pepper and salt and garnish with parsley leaves before serving hot.

Hearty Salad Medley

This is a hearty yet quick and easy salad recipe. A quick combination of these ingredients will deliver a colorful presentation of the vegetables.

MAKES: 2 servings
PREPARATION TIME: 10 minutes

---

2 heads Red Leaf Lettuce, torn into bite-size pieces
3 Carrots, peeled and spiralized
1 bunch Chives, coarsely chopped
2 Cucumbers, spiralized
3 large Tomatoes, chopped into cubes
1 medium Avocado, chopped into cubes
½ cup Pumpkin Seeds, roasted
1 tablespoon Olive Oil
½ teaspoon Lemon Juice
Sea Salt, to taste

Directions

1. In a bowl, mix olive oil, lemon juice, sea salt and black pepper. Toss the

remaining ingredients together in a large bowl and dress with the olive oil mixture. Serve immediately.

Hot Squash Turkey Stew

This appetizing meal may soon become one of your favorites. Enjoy this tasty and nutritious dish whenever you want a healthy turkey meal.

MAKES: 2 servings
PREPARATION TIME: 15 minutes
COOKING TIME: 30 minutes

½ Head Broccoli, chopped roughly
1 tablespoon Extra Virgin Coconut Oil
½ Onion, chopped
1 Garlic Clove, minced
½ pound (226g) Grass-Fed Boneless Turkey
Cutlet, sliced thinly
1 Jalapeño Pepper, seeded and chopped
2 cups Low-sodium Chicken Broth
1 Summer Squash, spiralized
1 teaspoon Ground Red Chili
Sea Salt, to taste
Freshly Ground Black Pepper, to taste

Directions

1. Add the broccoli to a large pan of boiling water. Cover and simmer for about 10 minutes. Remove from heat and drain before letting it cool.

2. In a non-stick skillet, heat the coconut oil on a medium heat. Add the onion and sauté for about 5 minutes. Add the garlic and jalapeño pepper, and sauté for 1 minute. Add the turkey and stir fry for about 5 minutes.

3. In a blender, add the broccoli and broth, and blend until smooth. Transfer the broccoli mixture into the pan.

4. Reduce the heat to low. Stir in the summer squash and seasonings and cook for about 7 minutes. Serve immediately.

Yellow Squash Casserole

This tasty yellow squash casserole recipe is quite a simple meal and offers heart health benefits.

MAKES: 3-4 servings
PREPARATION TIME: 15 minutes
COOKING TIME: 30 minutes

---

3 Yellow Squash, spiralized
2 tablespoons Fresh Basil, chopped
1 large Onion, chopped
2 tablespoons Extra Virgin Coconut Oil
2 tablespoons Almond Butter
3 Organic Eggs, beaten
Freshly Ground Black Pepper, to taste
Sea Salt, to taste

Directions

1. In a large skillet, add the coconut oil and onion and cook for about 1 minute.
2. Steam the yellow squash in a covered pot with water on medium flame until

the peel for about minutes. Drain any excess liquid after steaming and arrange the squash at the bottom of a greased oven-proof casserole dish. Spread the almond butter on top.

3. Preheat oven to 375 degrees Fahrenheit.

4. In a small bowl, add the basil, eggs, black pepper and sea salt. Stir well to combine. Pour this mixture over the squash in the casserole dish.

5. Bake in a preheated oven for approximately 25 minutes. Serve warm or at room temperature.

Breakfast Zoodle Quiche

These breakfast quiches are remarkably a great addition to your gluten-free breakfast routine. Sautéed kale and zucchinis makes these quiches a tasty and yummy treat.

MAKES: 2 servings
PREPARATION TIME: 10 minutes
COOKING TIME: 25 minutes

---

2 teaspoons Extra Virgin Coconut Oil
1 Zucchini, spiralized and trimmed into 1-inch pieces
1 cup Kale, trimmed and torn
2 Organic Eggs
½ teaspoon Dried Rosemary, crushed
Sea Salt, to taste
Black Pepper, to taste
2 tablespoons Nut Butter (Almond, Pecan or Walnut)
½ tablespoon Organic Unsweetened Coconut Cream

Directions

1. Preheat the oven to 375 degrees F. Lightly grease a 6 cups muffins tray.
2. In a pan, heat oil on medium heat. Add zucchini and sauté for about 4 to 5 minutes.
3. Transfer the zucchini in a plate.
4. In the same pan, add kale and sauté for about 4 minutes or until just wilted. Take from heat.
5. In a bowl, add eggs, rosemary, sea salt and black pepper and beat well.
6. Add zucchini, kale, nut butter and coconut cream in egg mixture and mix until well combined.
7. Place the mixture in prepared muffins tray. Bake for about 21 minutes or until a toothpick inserted in the center comes out clean. Serve these zoodle quiches with your favorite protein.

Lamb Chops Combo

This lamb chops recipe makes a simply delicious and quick dinner or lunch meal. Enjoy the combination of zucchini and carrots with these succulent lamb chops.

MAKES: 4 servings
PREPARATION TIME: 10 minutes
COOKING TIME: 10 minutes

---

1 tablespoon Organic Extra Virgin Coconut Oil, divided
4 grass-fed Lamb Chops
1 Parsnip, peeled and spiralized
3 Zucchinis, spiralized
1 Onion, finely chopped
1 tablespoon Dried Thyme, crushed
1 tablespoon Dried Oregano, crushed
Sea Salt, to taste
Freshly Ground Black Pepper, to taste

Directions

1. In a non-stick skillet, heat oil on medium-low heat. Add chops and cook

for 4 to 5 minutes.

2. Add parsnip, zucchini, onion, thyme, oregano, salt and pepper and cook for about 4 minutes or until lamb chops are done completely.

3. Serve immediately with topping of fresh rosemary.

Curried Beef Stir-Fry

This curried ground beef stir-fry dish combines ground beef and summer squash to make a healthy and tasty meal. Enjoy the rich flavor in every bite.

MAKES: 2 servings
PREPARATION TIME: 10 minutes
COOKING TIME: 15 minutes

---

1 tablespoon Extra Virgin Olive Oil
1 Onion, finely chopped
2 Garlic Cloves, minced
¼ teaspoon Fresh Ginger, minced
½ pound (226 grams) Grass-fed Lean Ground Beef
1 small Tomato, finely chopped
1 medium Summer Squash, spiralized
2 tablespoons Fresh Parsley
Sea Salt, to taste
Freshly Ground Black pepper, to taste
1 teaspoon Turmeric Powder
½ teaspoon Coriander Powder
½ teaspoon Cumin Powder
½ teaspoon Smoked Paprika

Directions

1. In a non-stick skillet, heat olive oil on medium heat.
2. Add onion and sauté for about 4 minutes. Add garlic and ginger and sauté for 1 minute more.
3. Add ground beef and cook for about 7 minutes.
4. Stir in tomato, summer squash, parsley and all the spices. Reduce the heat to medium-low. Cover and cook for about 2 minutes or until squash become tender but not mushy.
5. Serve immediately.

Creamy Stew Chicken

Enjoy this creamy stew chicken dish which is completely tasty and may remind you of a hearty chicken stew. This sumptuous stew combines chicken thighs and spiralized carrots with an array of interesting spices.

MAKES: 2 servings
PREPARATION TIME: 10 minutes
COOKING TIME: 40 minutes

---

1 tablespoon Extra Virgin Olive Oil
1 White Onion, chopped
2 Garlic Cloves, chopped finely
2 free-range Boneless Chicken Thighs, cubed
1½ cups Homemade Chicken Broth
1 cup Homemade Tomato Puree
¼ teaspoon Coriander Powder
¼ teaspoon Cumin Powder
Chili powder, to taste
2 tablespoons Almond Butter
2 Carrots, peeled and spiralized
1 Parsnip, peeled and spiralized
Sea Salt, to taste

Directions

1. In a large pan, olive oil on medium heat. Add onion and sauté for about 4 minutes. Add garlic and sauté for 1 minute more.
2. Add chicken thighs and cook for 4 to 5 minutes. Add remaining all ingredients except almond butter and carrots.
3. Bring to a boil and reduce the heat to medium-low. Cover and simmer for about 18 minutes. Then uncover and simmer for about 10 minutes or until the liquid becomes thickened.
4. In the last 2 minutes, add almond butter, carrots and parsnip then stir until well combined.
5. Garnish this stew with chopped fresh parsley leaves.

Spaghetti & Chicken Balls

This delicious dish presents an exciting chicken meatball meal that is nicely combined with zucchini pasta for a nice taste and flavor.

MAKES: 2 servings
PREPARATION TIME: 10 minutes
COOKING TIME: 40 minutes

For Chicken Meatballs

1 pound (453 grams) free-range Ground Chicken
2 Organic Eggs, beaten
½ cup + 2 tablespoons Almond Flour
1 small Onion, finely chopped
½ teaspoon Fresh Ginger, minced
2 teaspoons Curry Powder
Pinch of Cayenne Pepper
Sea Salt, to taste
Freshly Ground Black Pepper, to taste

For Spaghetti and Sauce

2 tablespoons Organic Extra-virgin Coconut Oil
1 small Onion, diced
1 Garlic Clove, minced

1 teaspoon Fresh Ginger, minced
2 cups Organic Coconut Milk
1 cup Homemade Chicken Broth
3 teaspoons Curry Powder
I teaspoon Cumin Powder
1 teaspoon Coriander Powder
2 Zucchinis, spiralized

Directions

1. In a large bowl, add all chicken meatballs ingredients and mix until well combined. Make balls from chicken mixture according to desired size.
2. In a skillet, heat coconut oil on medium heat. Add onion and sauté for about 3 minutes.
3. Add garlic and ginger and sauté for 1 minute more. Add chicken meatballs and cook for 3 to 4 minutes from all sides.
4. Add remaining curry sauce ingredients, except the zucchini and mix well.
5. Bring to a boil and reduce the heat to

medium-low.

6. Add zucchini and cover and simmer for about 4 minutes or until the sauce becomes thick.

7. Garnish this dish with freshly chopped parsley.

Italian Baked Chicken & Squash

This is a very filling meal and would be a good choice for a healthy and quick chicken meal.

MAKES: 4 servings
PREPARATION TIME: 10 minutes
COOKING TIME: 20 minutes

---

4 free-range boneless Chicken Thighs
2 Summer Squash, spiralized
2 Yellow Squash, spiralized
2 Heads Cauliflower, cut in florets
1 tablespoon Italian Seasoning
1 teaspoon Garlic Powder
Sea Salt, to taste
Freshly Ground Black Pepper, to taste
2 tablespoons Raw Coconut Vinegar
¼ cup Organic Extra-virgin Coconut Oil

Directions

1. Preheat the oven to 375 degrees F. Line a baking dish with parchment paper.
2. Place all ingredients in baking dish and

toss to coat well.

3. Bake for 20 minutes. Serve as desired.

Crispy Mint Salad

This minty fresh salad may go well with your lunch or dinner. It is topped with fresh mint leaves which deliver a double dose of the refreshing mint flavor.

MAKES: 2 servings
PREPARATION TIME: 10 minutes (Plus time for refrigeration)

---

2 Carrots, spiralized
1 cup Green Grape Tomatoes
½ small Red Onion, sliced thinly
1 tablespoon diced Fresh Cilantro Leaves
1 tablespoon Fresh Mint Leaves, minced finely
1 Garlic Clove, minced
1 tablespoon Coconut Vinegar
2 tablespoons Olive Oil
Sea Salt, to taste
Freshly Ground Black Pepper, to taste
1 cup Baby Spinach Leaves

Directions

1. In a large bowl add all of the ingredients, except for the spinach. Toss the ingredients together, then refrigerate for at least 1 hour.
2. While serving, place the spinach in a large serving bowl and mix in the refrigerated carrot mixture. Top with some more fresh mint leaves.

Nutty Chicken Salad

This interesting and inspirational chicken salad may go well as a side salad or for a light dinner or lunch dish. It is nicely topped with nuts to deliver extra protein nutrition.

MAKES: 2 servings
PREPARATION TIME: 20 minutes

---

2 medium Cucumbers, spiralized and gently pat dried with paper towels
1 small Avocado, peeled, pitted and diced
2 cooked grass-fed Boneless Chicken Breasts, shredded or cubed
1 tablespoons Extra Virgin Olive Oil
1 tablespoons Fresh Lime or Lemon juice
1 small Sweet Onion, chopped
1 Garlic Clove, minced
1 tablespoon minced Parsley Leaves
Sea Salt, to taste
Freshly Ground Black Pepper, to taste
2 tablespoons Almonds, chopped

Directions

1. In a large serving bowl, mix together the spiralized cucumber, avocado and chicken.
2. In a food processor, add all of the remaining ingredients, except for the almonds, and pulse until pureed. Pour the dressing over the cucumber mixture and gently toss to coat.
3. Top with the almonds and serve.

Garlic & Potato Shrimp

This interesting recipe has a delicate mix of sweet potato pasta with a garlic flavored shrimp. It will be a great addition to a dinner or lunch menu.

MAKES: 2 servings
PREPARATION TIME: 20 minutes
COOKING TIME: 18 minutes

---

1 tablespoon Organic Extra-Virgin Olive Oil
2 Garlic Cloves, minced
1 cup Fresh Tomatoes, finely chopped
2 tablespoons Homemade Vegetable Broth
2 tablespoons Kalamata Olives, pitted and halved
1 tablespoon Fresh Cilantro, chopped
Pinch of Cayenne Pepper
Sea Salt, to taste
Freshly Ground Black Pepper, to taste
2 small-medium Sweet Potatoes, peeled and spiralized
8 medium Shrimp, peeled and deveined

Directions

1. In a medium skillet, heat the olive oil on a medium-low heat. Sauté the garlic for 1 minute. Add the tomatoes and cook for about 2 minutes while also crushing them. Add the broth, olives, cilantro, cayenne pepper, salt and black pepper. Cook, stirring occasionally, for 5 minutes.
2. Stir in the spiralized sweet potatoes. Cover and cook for 5 minutes, tossing once after 2 minutes. Gently stir in the shrimp. Cover and cook for a further 5 minutes.
3. Serve warm.

9

IT'S A WIN-WIN APPROACH

Unquestionably, the overall health benefits of using the Veggetti to make inspiringly healthy low carb meals are limitless. So, even if you don't have a reason to go gluten-free, by having fewer carbs and fats in your diet you'll be bound to improve your overall health. Besides, it's fun to prepare sumptuous meals from vegetable spaghetti that your family and friends will love. Essentially, this cookbook will be a useful "go-to" resource to help you along your exciting veggie pasta journey.

For many, there is sometimes a challenge to always come up with new and interesting cooking ideas for the Veggetti. Before long, boredom and demotivation to use this interestingly new kitchen gadget sometimes becomes a reality. But it doesn't have to be. So, if you've been struggling to come up with new and inspiring spiralizer recipes, your struggles are over. Furthermore, if these recipes have enhanced my health and the health of others, then it is very likely that it will also improve yours. In the end, the overall benefits of eating vegetable spaghetti noodles are far more beneficial than eating any regular pasta dish.

Again, I thank you for choosing my cookbook. If you find it to be helpful, I would appreciate if you would let other readers know about it. Using your Veggetti to create healthy vegetable spaghetti meals is a win-win approach to good health!

Yours in health,
Stacy Hill